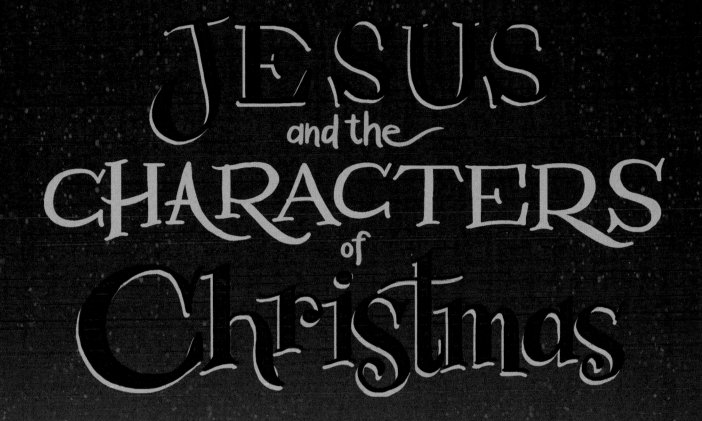

JESUS
and the
CHARACTERS
of
Christmas

Daniel Darling
Art by Guy Wolek

HARVEST
Kids

HARVEST HOUSE PUBLISHERS
EUGENE, OREGON

All Scripture quotations are taken from the Holy Bible, New Living Translation, copyright © 1996, 2004, 2015 by Tyndale House Foundation. Used by permission of Tyndale House Publishers, Inc., Carol Stream, Illinois 60188. All rights reserved.

Published in association with the literary agency of Wolgemuth & Associates

Cover hand lettering and design by Juicebox Designs
Interior design by Nicole Dougherty
Author photo © by Lifetouch. Used by permission.

For bulk, special sales, or ministry purchases, please call 1-800-547-8979.
Email: Customerservice@hhpbooks.com

This logo is a federally registered trademark of the Hawkins Children's LLC. Harvest House Publishers, Inc., is the exclusive licensee of this trademark.

Based on *The Characters of Christmas* by Daniel Darling (Moody Publishers, 2019)

Jesus and the Characters of Christmas
Text copyright © 2023 by Daniel Darling
Artwork © 2023 by Guy Wolek
Published by Harvest House Publishers
Eugene, Oregon 97408
www.harvesthousepublishers.com

ISBN 978-0-7369-8794-3 (hardcover)
Library of Congress Control Number: 2023931127

Printed in China

23 24 25 26 27 28 29 30 31 / LP / 10 9 8 7 6 5 4 3 2 1

But you, O Bethlehem Ephrathah,
are only a small village among all the people of Judah.
Yet a ruler of Israel,
whose origins are in the distant past,
will come from you on my behalf.

. . . And you are to name him Jesus, for he will save his people.

MICAH 5:2 *and* MATTHEW 1:21

What's your favorite story?

The Bible is filled with all sorts of true and amazing stories!
Stories about . . .

battles and underdogs,

adventures and friendship,

kings and queens!

But do you know the grandest story of all?
It's the story of **Jesus**, the Son of God.
Born among unlikely people in an unlikely place,
He would one day save the world.

Angels show up all throughout the Christmas story. You couldn't tell it without them.

Keep a lookout because the
angels have an important job.

Angels are special beings created by God.
And they have superpowers!

Sometimes they use those powers
to teach or guide or protect people.

They also share God's messages with others.

The angels are only a few of the many
unexpected characters in Jesus's story.

Jesus is kind and loving and perfect.

But others in His story are just normal people like you and me.

Here are some of Jesus's great-great-great-great
(add a whole bunch more "greats") grandparents:

Abraham struggled
but believed
God's promises.

David defeated a giant
and was crowned king
but made big mistakes.

Rahab had a dark past but believed in God's promise to save and rescue those who are far from Him.

Ruth was from Moab, a country that opposed God's people. But Ruth was faithful, and God used her too.

Thankfully, God had a plan for these misfits all along.

"A Messiah is coming to save the world!"
God's messengers declared.

So the people hoped and waited. Waited and hoped.

Finally, after four hundred years of silence, on an ordinary day,
God revealed a big part of His amazing story . . .

to one of the most unlikely people you could imagine.

A simple young girl named **Mary** lived in the little town of Nazareth.

Mary wasn't famous or rich. People probably thought she wasn't noteworthy at all.

But God doesn't care about what other people think. He doesn't care if people have lots of money or cool toys or fancy clothes.

God uses regular, ordinary people to do incredible things.
Mary was one of those people.

"*Greetings, favored one!*" an angel said to Mary.

The angel told Mary that she would become pregnant by God's Spirit and give birth to the Savior of the entire world. The Son of God would leave heaven and become a human—a tiny baby!

Really? Mary, a simple girl from a nowhere place,
would be the mother of God's Son?
But Mary listened and believed.

One day, she would see her son on a cruel cross.
But she would also see Him rise again on the third day.

Zechariah and Elizabeth had always wanted a baby.
But at their old age, having a baby now seemed impossible.

Then one day, an angel appeared in the temple
where Zechariah was a priest.

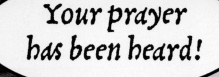

The angel said Elizabeth would have a baby
who would prepare the way for the Savior.

Zechariah doubted. But surprise—the angel was right!

Months later, Mary went to visit her cousin Elizabeth.
As Mary told Elizabeth about Jesus, the baby inside
Elizabeth leaped with joy at the news. Hooray!

Joseph was a carpenter and a descendant of King David.

He was engaged to Mary when he found out she was pregnant.

Had Mary done something wrong?
Joseph was confused. What would he do?

An angel came to Joseph in a dream explaining
that Mary would give birth to God's Son.

Joseph took Mary as his wife
and agreed to be Jesus's dad on earth.

This lowly carpenter would help raise the Son of God.
He would obey God and put the needs of
Jesus and Mary ahead of his own.

Soon the king in Rome told every person in Israel
to travel back to their hometown to be counted.

So Mary and Joseph made their way
to the tiny town of Bethlehem.

After a loooooong journey, Mary and Joseph arrived in Bethlehem.

They must have been really tired and ready to rest. But there was a problem . . .

Thankfully, they were given a place
to rest—although it was probably
pretty dirty and smelly.

Baby Jesus was wrapped in cloths and
laid in a manger—a feeding box for animals.
Not exactly where you'd expect the King of
all kings to spend the night of His birth!

On that same night, some **shepherds** were watching their sheep when suddenly an angel appeared!

Soon a bunch *more* angels popped into the sky,
praising God for this baby King.

The shepherds went out right away to find Jesus.
Then they spread the exciting news all around town!

These poor shepherds were the first people to find out
about the most incredible event in the history of the world.

But Jesus didn't come just for famous or fancy people.
Jesus came for outsiders too.

Meanwhile, some very smart and important men
from the East looked up in the sky and saw a new star.

A king has
been born!

These **wise men** probably didn't look or talk like most people
did who lived around Jesus. But God placed this star in the sky
so they could follow it and come worship this new King—because
Jesus came to save people from all over the world.

The wise men offered Jesus
gifts of gold, frankincense, and myrrh.

They were very important men, but they bowed before
this little boy because they knew He was the Son of God.
This is what everyone should do at Christmas—worship Jesus.

All these characters make up some of Jesus's story.

Would you believe that **you** can be part of Jesus's story too?

It's true!

No matter where you're from, who you are, or what you do, you can play a role in the greatest story ever. You can be part of God's family when you do like **Mary** did and believe Jesus paid for your sins, and when you do like the **wise men** did and bow down and worship Him as Lord.

So, go! Like the **shepherds**, share the amazing story of our Savior, inviting even more unlikely characters to be part of the story too.

About the Author

Daniel Darling is the director of the Land Center for Cultural Engagement and the bestselling author of several books, including *The Characters of Christmas*; *The Biggest, Best Light*; and *The Dignity Revolution*. Dan is a columnist for *World* magazine and a contributor to *USA Today*. His work has been featured by *Christianity Today*, The Gospel Coalition, CNN, Fox, *Time*, *National Review*, and the *Washington Post*.

He is the host of a popular weekly podcast, *The Way Home*, where he interviews Christian leaders, politicians, and journalists.

Dan is a graduate of Southern Baptist Theological Seminary. He and his wife, Angela, have four children and reside in the Nashville, Tennessee, area. They attend Green Hill Church, where Dan serves as pastor of teaching and discipleship.

There's More for You to Discover...

This children's book is based on the bestselling version for adults. Increase your knowledge of the influential yet often overlooked people in the Christmas story. Ideal for personal study or as a gift for loved ones.

Discover *The Characters of Christmas* at MoodyPublishers.com or wherever books are sold.

THE
CHARACTERS
of CHRISTMAS

DANIEL DARLING